Making it work for you!

The Potent Force of the Universe

Lester Sumrall

Unless otherwise indicated,
all Scripture quotations are taken from
the *King James Version* of the Bible.

ISBN O-937580-85-6
Set up and printed 1985
Published by LeSEA Publishing Company
P.O. Box 12
South Bend, Indiana 46624

CONTENTS

Other books by Lester Sumrall:

LeSEA Publishing Co.

- Dominion Is Yours
- Genesis, Crucible of the Universe
- Paul, Man of the Millennia
- The Total Man
- The Human Body
- The Human Soul
- The Human Spirit
- The Will—The Potent Force Of The Universe
- The Battle Of The Ages
- Imagination

Nelson Publishing Co.

- Demons The Answer Book
- Grief, You Can Conquer It
- Hostility
- My Story To His Glory
- 60 Things God Said About Sex
- Supernatural Principalities & Powers
- The Cup Of Life
- The Names Of God
- The Reality Of Angels
- Where Was God When Pagan Religions Began?
- Jerusalem, Where Empires Die-- Will America Die At Jerusalem?

Harrison House

- Faith To Change The World
- Gifts & Ministries of the Holy Spirit
- Jihad—The Holy War
- Unprovoked Murder
- Victory & Dominion Over Fear
- 101 Questions & Answers On Demon Power

1

WHAT IS WILL?

WILL is a MAJOR FORCE in the universe. If you have a James Strong Concordance, you will notice that the words *will, willfully,* and *willingly* take up about 12 pages of the concordance. In counting down the columns, I discovered each page had about 360 references, which is 4320 references to *will.* It looks like God is trying to get our attention when he puts 4320 references on any subject in the Bible.

I have spent considerable time in seeking God and thinking about the WILL. I trust you will join me with your heart open, with your spirit open, and let's discover things about yourself and about God.

WHO HAS WILL?

There are at least six distinct creatures in our universe who possess will, or willpower. Willpower is a dominant fact regarding destiny for rational persons. You are what you are by will. You will spend eternity in heaven or hell by your will.

The human will is one-third of his human soulical personality. God created Adam a **three-dimensional person.** He was a spirit, a soul, and a body. In this study we are reaching into a dimension of soul. The soul has three divisions but we are reaching into just one of them. As human persons we should know what willpower is, where it generates from, what causes it to function, and what it will do for us. We must learn to control willpower.

God wants us to understand the force of willpower, to identify it as it functions. He wants us to know by divine decree that you and I can be victorious in every department of our created being.

We will observe that God, the Creator of all things, possesses and has willpower.

He is the originator of willpower, and so when we find out what willpower is in God, we can see what willpower is to you.

We shall observe that Jesus Christ, God's only begotten Son, possessed tremendous willpower. He functioned in willpower, and if we see this then we can say, "The willpower that was in the Lord Jesus Christ can function in my life." So you will be able to coordinate the truth of willpower by observing it first in God the Father, and then in God the Son.

We also seek to penetrate the third entity of the Holy Trinity, the Holy Spirit, and learn that He exerts amazing and mighty willpower.

We will also study other rational creatures such as the entities called angels—heavenly persons and heavenly beings—and learn that they possess willpower. These entities, called angels, obey God by option. They do not have to obey God; they *will* to obey God. They are not slaves; they are not without opinion, and they are not without decision.

Everytime God speaks they exert willpower as to obey or disobey.

On the negative side, all demons possess willpower and the devil has strong willpower. Demons use their willpower to combat the purpose of God in the universe.

When you observe willpower in such a panoramic view from God the Father, even to Satan, and all between, you may say, "Well, why didn't I know that before?" You cannot live a victorious Christian life without having some recognition that deep down within you are forces that really make you. Those forces, if they are directed by God, lead you in the right direction. Those forces, dominated by the devil, will put you on the wrong road.

GOD CREATED THE WILL IN MAN

MAN, the Homo sapiens that God created and placed upon planet Earth, is the apex of all of God's creation. Man was endowed with sovereign willpower. This endowment and this power was granted unto man by divine prerogative.

God said, "I will create this person and call him 'man.' I will give him willpower." In doing so, God made him a creature of judgment. He made him a creature of understanding. He made him a creature of decision. You do not have to go straight ahead; you can go backwards if you want to. You do not have to turn to the right, you can go to the left if you want to. God places in you the amazing volitional strengths and anointings and powers of what we call WILL.

Now when God granted you this, He determined that He would never violate it. Sometimes you say, "Why didn't God stop Hitler? Why didn't God stop Stalin? Why doesn't God stop Castro? Why doesn't God stop this, that, and the other? God has granted us decision power. He has granted us willpower, and God will not violate it. He will let you eventually be lost if you want to be. God will not violate man's willpower.

The devil cannot violate it. I have talked to some of the most extreme cases of devil possession on the face of the earth, and every one of them told me that they did not have to obey the devil. They did as they pleased. They exerted willpower.

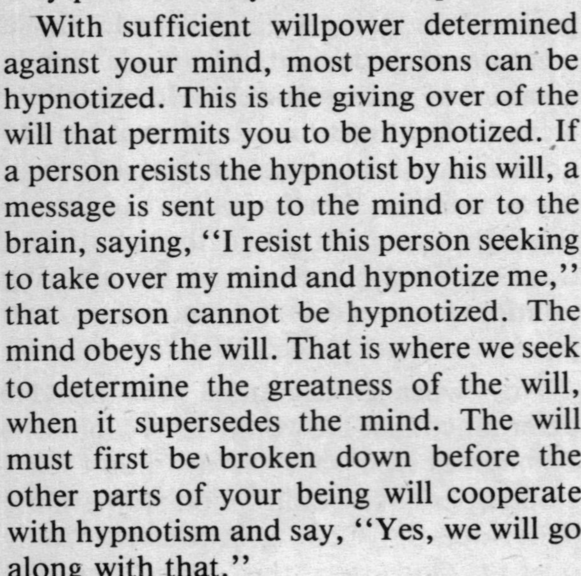

With sufficient willpower determined against your mind, most persons can be hypnotized. This is the giving over of the will that permits you to be hypnotized. If a person resists the hypnotist by his will, a message is sent up to the mind or to the brain, saying, "I resist this person seeking to take over my mind and hypnotize me," that person cannot be hypnotized. The mind obeys the will. That is where we seek to determine the greatness of the will, when it supersedes the mind. The will must first be broken down before the other parts of your being will cooperate with hypnotism and say, "Yes, we will go along with that."

The will cannot be weighed on a scale. You cannot measure the will. Will is different from your corporeal person, such as your eyes, your hands, your feet. These can be seen and felt, but your will goes beyond that part of your total personality. It is a strong thing that governs. It governs your hands and your feet and your seeing and your hearing and so forth. Man is blessed by his Creator as possessing a three-fold personality. The will is a third part of your soulical being. Your soulical being is your mind, your emotions, and your will. The will can be destroyed, polluted, and broken down with alcohol or drugs etc. Then a human person cannot exercise will as God created it to function. Will is to be a protected part of your personality.

When man is using or operating in his **soulical parts,** he is using his **mind,** or he is using his **emotions,** or he is using his **will.** He can be using two parts or even three parts of his soul at the same time. For example, he can be using his mind and his will, functioning simultaneously. He wills to do something, the idea is conveyed to the mind, and the mind carries it out. It can be something of a fantastic nature and the emotions would jump in and say, "Ah, I'm glad, I'm glad, I'm glad." Then he would have all three of his soulical portions functioning at one time. When man is not functioning by his mind, or if he is not functioning by his emotions, for sure he is operating in the area of his will. He wills to do a certain thing. So his will is in action at that point, determining what he will be in all the parts of his total personality.

The will can be moved and activated by three elements.

1) By divine **spiritual** power
2) By **human** power
3) By **demonic** power

This means the will of man can be motivated by God, by man himself, or by satanic forces.

To analyze the will we must observe that it is a power that is manifested by intelligence; whether it is a deity, whether it is in angels, in mankind, or in devils. *Without intelligence there is no will.*

WISH

To will is to wish, and is related to willingness, or an assent to perform. If you do not will to do a thing, you become unwilling. That means that your will goes into reverse. For example, God said to me, "Will you go to Manila, Philippines, and be a missionary?" I said, "I will." I didn't say, "I think, or feel." I said, "I will." So God's will and my will got together and I took my family to the Philippines. My reward was that God gave us the greatest revival we have ever seen in our lives. We saw 150,000 people publicly accept Christ.

HOPE

To will is also *to hope.* The will has power to invade the future with a new and a fresh experience. Hope is a strong force. It is a force to determine our destiny. When that hope surges within you, by the powers of your will, things begin to change around you. You do not accept the status quo. You do not accept things as they are. Your will is the determining factor to say I am hoping for a better day, a better situation. Your will brings energy into action that causes a change.

AT WILL

What does the word "at will" mean? It means an intelligent creature moves and thinks in an uninhibited manner as he desires, or wishes, or feels. He does it "at will." This is a category of greatness and of potential life and strength and vigor that we can hardly imagine.

Do you realize that 90% of the world population today cannot function "at will"? They do not have the freedom.

This causes frustration because man is born of free will. God created him a free moral agent. He is in complete charge of his willfulness, either to follow God or not to follow God, to live peacefully or not to live peacefully. God has permitted him to have this tremendous force of will to be what the Lord has designed him for and wants him to be.

When we speak about being "at will" it means that an intelligent creature moves and thinks in an uninhibited way; that he has the right to do it and the power to do it.

Possibly man has never yet fathomed the depth of the intelligent will of a human person, or the complete will for humankind.

2

THE WILL OF GOD THE FATHER

What do we truly know about WILL in the person of God the Father who, in divine providence and wisdom, created WILL itself?

Jehovah God has will; **He created all the will in the universe.** When God created intelligent creatures He set them free through the mighty agency called WILL.

GOD'S WILL IN HEAVEN

In the gospel of Matthew 6:9-10, the disciples asked Jesus to teach them how to pray. He said, "After this manner therefore pray ye: Our Father. . ."

That is remarkable. God is not our boss or our dictator. He is our Father. The father image is a remarkable one.

"...which art in heaven, Hallowed be thy name. Thy kingdom come. Thy will be done in earth, as it is in heaven."

The will of God is done in heaven. **How can that will be identified here** on the face of the earth?

GOD'S WILL IN MAN

God the Father possesses will. In I Thessalonians 5:18 we find these words: "...for this is the will of God in Christ Jesus concerning you."

To all intelligent creatures God gave a will, which means He gave a part or a portion of Himself. On earth we have the will of God, the will of Christ, the will of the Holy Spirit, the will of angels, and the will of men; there is also the will of the devil and of demons.

GOD'S WILL IS NOT DIFFICULT

The first thing we must understand is that **the will of God for us is not difficult.**

That will distress some people who say, "My, but the will of God is so hard." It is the devil who speaks things like that.

In Psalm 40:8, David says, "I delight to do thy will, O my God: yea, thy law is within my heart."

David had discovered God's will, and he said, *"I delight to do it and find it within my heart."* How would one go about seeking to know the will of God the Father?

First, knowing that He is a father, you do not have to scream at Him, crying, "Oh, God, show me thy will!"

When I had three sons at home, if they came screaming downstairs in the morning while I was having a cup of coffee with my wife, saying, "What is your will, oh, Father? What is your will?" I would have said, "Right now, go back to bed and get some rest!"

Possibly God feels that way about some of us sometimes when we start screaming at Him. But knowing **the will of God is so simple and so easy.** All you have to do is understand His Fatherhood.

My three sons, though I do not know exactly where they are at this moment, are in my will because they are my sons. As God's children, we do what He wants us to do because we are His children. You do not have to worry - "Oh, am I in the will of God?" Yes, because you are born into the family. Unless you have violated His will, you are in His will. All Christians are in the will of God, unless they have rebelled against His will. All unsaved people are out of the will of God, for the simple reason they are in a state of rebellion against God.

God will teach us how to do His will. In Psalm 143:10, it says, "Teach me to do thy will; for thou art my God: (that is a good confession to make) thy spirit is good; lead me into the land of uprightness." Here we find a man who had come to understand the will of God. He said, *"Teach me thy will;* for thou art my God: thy spirit is good."

Romans 12:2 says, "Be not conformed to this world." Non-conformity to the world means total dedication—that when we say, "Lord, we're going to serve you fully and completely and absolutely," then our will is subject to the will of God. Then we are walking in what we call "God's will."

In Ephesians 6:6 Paul says, "Not with eye-service, as men-pleasers; but as the servants of Christ, doing the will of God from the heart." That means down within us there is a will, and that will moves up through our emotions and up through our minds. We are determining, operating and functioning in the will of God from an inner source of power that comes to us through the new birth—as a gift from God.

GOD'S PERMISSIVE WILL

In studying "will" we find a remarkable situation—that God the Father has a **permissive will.** He has a strong will that says "do this" and He means it. He also has a permissive will. You make the decision, then you ask God to bless it. I must tell you that *multiplied millions live in the permissive will of God.*

When I was a boy growing up I often

lived in the permissive will of my parents—not in their full will, not in their delightful will. I would want to do something and they would say, "We do not want you to do it." I would say, "I want to do it," and their answer was, "Well, go ahead and do it." Sometimes it brought troubles, sorrows, and problems because my will was not subjective. The human will is wild until God gets hold of it and makes it subject to His will.

GOD'S PERFECT WILL

It is God's will that you be **saved.** It is God's will that you have **health.** It is not God's will for you to be sick. God's will is for us to be strong right up to the time we go to heaven. Moses was a beautiful example of the will of God. He lived 120 years and the last day he lived he climbed a mountain by himself. From the mountain he beheld the treasures of God, and the beauties of God for Israel. Then he gave up the ghost, and angels took him to heaven.

It is the will of God for you to make **quality decisions** in **your business, your**

family, in **your own life.** It is God's will that you be a very successful person upon the face of this earth.

As far as I know, since I was 17 years of age, I have walked in the will of God. I wanted His will. I **subjected my will to His will.** I did not go to the Philippines because I wanted to go. I did not come to South Bend, Indiana, to minister because I wanted to. I was born in New Orleans, Louisiana, and would much prefer living in a southern city. But God's will is to be accomplished. The reason I can teach these things is because I have been comforted by walking in the will of God for these many years. And by walking in the will of God, I can understand what God's will is concerning me, and what my will is concerning God. It is a resourceful life and a happy life. A blessed life.

LIVING IN GOD'S WILL

We receive what we are through the will of God. I Corinthians 1:1 says, "Paul, *called* to be an apostle of Jesus Christ *through the will of God...*"

Paul knew that he had received apostleship and ministry through the will of God.

That means that Paul's will became subservient to the Father's will and that he had position in the church through the will of God. Also in II Corinthians 1:1 it says, "Paul, an apostle of Jesus Christ by the will of God..."

All **spiritual leadership** and position should be **according to God's desires and knowledge of human need** and we should fit into that. We should be whatever our nation needs the most by the will of God.

The problem that I see in the word "will" is that we have used it so much that we do not know what "will" is. We cannot find the source of it. We cannot find the outflow of it. We are actually laboring in an unknown area.

Will originated in God. It was given to man. If we learn this we will know how to function in the will of God. We must learn to function in a will that has been made new, dedicated, set apart to carry out the "will of God on earth as it is in heaven."

THANKFULNESS IS GOD'S WILL

God's will is that we be thankful. I Thessalonians 5:18, "In every thing give thanks: for this is the will of God in Christ Jesus concerning you."

God desires thankfulness. It is God's will that you be grateful.

You would be amazed at how many people sit down to eat without giving thanks. Many people go to bed at night without thanking God for the day; most people begin their days without thanking God for the night.

Also people receive good things in their lives without saying, "Thank you, God." The will of God concerning you, the Bible says, is that you give thanks to God.

BEING SUBJECT TO THE WILL OF GOD

In Matthew 7:21, Jesus said, "Not every one that saith unto me, Lord, Lord, shall enter into the kingdom of heaven; but *he that doeth the will of my Father* which is in heaven."

The will of God has a relationship with your eternal destiny. **You cannot just do as you please!** You cannot just let your will run riot and expect to reach heaven.

Jesus said that what will get you to heaven is doing the will of the Father which is in heaven.

There are people living now whose lives are not subject to the will of God. Those who do as they please are living in their own will and in their own desires. Those people find themselves not in the proper relationship with the Most High God. The will of God the Father is that you know His will and perform it.

KNOWING GOD AND HIS WILL

It is the will of God that all men have a keen knowledge of God. I Timothy 2:4, "Who will have all men to be saved, and to come unto the knowledge of the truth."

It is the will of God that we accept the Great Commission "...Go ye into all the world, and preach the gospel to every creature. He that believeth and is baptized shall be saved; but he that believeth not shall be damned. And these signs shall follow them that believe; In my name shall they cast out devils..." (Mark 16:15-17)

The will of God is that you and I be pioneers in our generation throughout the earth delivering the message of truth, the message of power, the message of eternal salvation.

Your willpower has to rise up within you and say, "*I will walk* in the WILL of *the Lord!*"

3

THE WILL OF JESUS CHRIST

We have now come to the **will of Jesus Christ.**

Really, we should go back before He was born, because He willed to come to Planet Earth and be born of the virgin Mary. His will began before His appearance on Planet Earth.

The Lord Jesus possessed divine free will, or as the Son of God, royal free will. It is recorded in the Gospels that Jesus said "I will" at least sixty times. Something within Him had a determining factor. Something within Him had a guiding force. It is called WILL. Jesus exercised what we call "free will." He did not have to do the things that He did. He did not have to heal the sick; He did not have to feed the hungry. He had **free will.**

Jesus Christ went to the cross freely. When Pilate said, "Don't you know that I can kill you?" He said, "No, you cannot do anything unless it be the will of God."

Jesus said, "Don't you realize I can call legions of angels who would set me free?" He willfully went to the cross.

It was the will of Jesus that gave Him a source of energy to achieve world redemption. He *willed* to save the world. By this will He drove His body to the cross; He drove His spirit to the cross by His willpower. Jesus said in Luke 22:42, "Father, if thou be willing, remove this cup from me: nevertheless not my will, but thine, be done." **Jesus was living in the will of the Father.**

Christ revealed God's will in His life. The beginning of this revealing of the will of God is found in Luke 2:49. Jesus was speaking to His own parents, "How is it that ye sought me? wist ye not (or didn't you know?) that I must be about my

Father's business?" When Jesus was twelve years of age, He wanted His parents to know there was a will beyond His will.

Christ was coordinating His will at twelve years of age. I do not think you can be too young to be functioning and working in the will of God for your life.

Beginning there, Jesus desired that His own will would not be performed. He knew that the Father in heaven had a will greater, more magnificent, more wonderful than the will of man. Jesus chose that His will would coordinate with the will of the Father. He knew that He had come to perform the will of the Father on the face of this earth. John 5:30 says, "I can of mine own self do nothing: as I hear, I judge: my judgment is just; *because I seek not mine own will* but the will of the Father which hath sent me."

That is about as strong a verse as you can find in the Bible. It means Christ had a will, and it could have been opposite to the plan of God, but He said, "I will not seek my will, but the will of the Father who sent me."

Evidently the **superior will of the universe is in the Father.** For us to do the will of God is the greatest achievement on the face of this earth. We must seek the will of God, we must find the will of God, and then we must coordinate it with our will. We should not say, "I do not want to do this, but I will do it anyway." That is not what God wants at all.

The perfect will of God flows out of us spontaneously, like an artesian well flowing with living water. God is desiring that you will have His ultimate will coming joyfully out of your heart as Christ had.

Christ entered human history to teach mankind how to perform God's will. That is the reason He was born. Hebrews 10:7-10 says, "Then said I, Lo, I come (in the volume of the book it is written of me,) to **do thy will,** O God. Above when he said, Sacrifice and offering and burnt offerings and offering for sin thou wouldest not, neither hadst pleasure therein; which are offered by the law; Then said he, Lo, I come to do thy will, O God. He taketh away the first, that he may establish the second. By the which will we are sanctified through the offering of the body of Jesus Christ once *for all.*"

So for sure, Christ entered human history to teach mankind—you and me—how we can perform the will of God.

JESUS LIVED BY GOD'S WILL

When you survey the life of Christ, you see that from His birth in Bethlehem, His life in Nazareth, and His traveling about all over that nation doing good, bringing healing, love, and all kinds of blessings to those people, that He was performing not a human will, but He was performing a divine mission. John 10:10, "For I am come that they might have life, and that they might have it more abundantly." He said in John 9:4, "I must work the works of him that sent me, while it is day: for the night cometh, when no man can work." Jesus had within Him, instilled deep within Him, a desire to perform only the will of God the Father.

Christ revealed a beautiful relationship of His will in the area of people that are sick. Matthew 8:3 says, "And Jesus put forth his hand, and touched him, saying, I will; be thou clean. And immediately his leprosy was cleansed."

Here was a man that sure missed Jesus. He came up to Him and said, "Master, I know that you could heal me if you will." He believed in Jesus' power but not His love. He was really speaking in unbelief. Jesus turned and said, "I will, be thou cleansed." The **human will** was **desire.** The **divine will** was pouring forth its **life.**

DIRECTION OF JESUS' WILL

What functioned in directing the will in Jesus? First, I would say His love. Christ came to reveal a divine attitude. God is love, so **He came to reveal God.** The will in the life of Jesus functioned through a spirit-life within Him called **love.**

Will could also be *compassion.* In His will, Christ suffered with humankind! He hurt with humankind; He cared for humankind. This is compassion. **So His will functioned out of compassion, out of love.**

Christ was the moving, walking, talking, and **living will of God,** and He demonstrated that will.

Christ demonstrated the will of the Father in labors; He slept at night on the ground—He had no bed. He walked many miles over rough terrain—He had no animal to ride. There were times He was hungry; there were times He was thirsty. He did not have to do that, but He willed to do it. He desired within Himself to do it.

In this area His mind could have said, "Do it;" His emotions could have said, "Do it;" and the will could have stopped and balked. On the other hand, His will could say, "Do it;" His emotions could say, "Oh, it's too hard;" His mind could say, "Hey, this is too much work;" but His will would win because the WILL is the **strongest force in the human person.**

Jesus demonstrated the great will of heaven, the will of God the Father, and He was revealing it through His attitude of life, love, and labors.

Christ was revealing what will means down on the inside of Christians, rising up in strength, in blessing, and in health.

One of the greatest aspects of Jesus' demonstrating the *will of God* was in His *forgiveness.* He willed to forgive people. It is divine to forgive. Christ harbored no

☐ My payment for $__________ is enclosed
☐ CHECK ☐ VISA ☐ MASTERCARD

____
SIGNATURE OF CARDHOLDER

______________ ______/______/______
INTERBANK NUMBER EXPIRATION DATE

______ / ______ / ______ / ______
CREDIT CARD NUMBER

NAME ______________________________

STREET ______________________________

STATE ____________________ ZIP__________

PHONE NUMBER ______________________

☐ My payment for $__________ is enclosed
☐ CHECK ☐ VISA ☐ MASTERCARD

____
SIGNATURE OF CARDHOLDER

______________ ______/______/______
INTERBANK NUMBER EXPIRATION DATE

______ / ______ / ______ / ______
CREDIT CARD NUMBER

NAME ______________________________

STREET ______________________________

STATE ____________________ ZIP__________

PHONE NUMBER ______________________

☐ My payment for $__________ is enclosed
☐ CHECK ☐ VISA ☐ MASTERCARD

____
SIGNATURE OF CARDHOLDER

______________ ______/______/______
INTERBANK NUMBER EXPIRATION DATE

______ / ______ / ______ / ______
CREDIT CARD NUMBER

NAME ______________________________

STREET ______________________________

STATE ____________________ ZIP__________

PHONE NUMBER ______________________

24-Hour Prayer Phone
(219) 291-1010

grudges; Christ harbored no hates; Christ harbored no unforgiveness. When Judas came to kiss Him, which was the kiss of betrayal, Jesus said, "Friend, what can I do for you?" He knew what he was going to do. He had already gone through the prayer in the garden. When Peter cursed and said that he had never heard of Jesus and did not know Him, Jesus said, "Call Peter back and I'll forgive him." He would have forgiven Judas if Judas had come and asked forgiveness, but he didn't want to come.

Will is demonstrated when you are a baby. The wildest of tantrums is willpower. It is not mental power; it is not emotional power; it is willpower. We often talk about "having to break his will." I do not know that that is a good word; you do not want to break anything—you want it to flow in God.

Jesus came to this earth to demonstrate that a human person could walk this earth and yet be in the will of God. Christ said, "I will be the perfect example of living and working in the will of God."

4

THE WILL OF THE HOLY GHOST

Jesus said He would send *another Comforter.* John 14:16, "And I will pray the Father, and he shall give you another Comforter, that he may abide with you for ever."

That meant He was a comforter, the Holy Ghost would also be a comforter.

Jesus said that He (the Holy Ghost) would teach you all things. Luke 12:12, "For the Holy Ghost shall teach you in the same hour what ye ought to say."

Christ said that the Holy Ghost will bring to remembrance things that are past.

Jesus said that He will guide you. That speaks of a person, not of an "it", or an influence. So we are dealing with the will of the PERSON of the Holy Ghost. You ought to write it down that way, then you will have it correct.

In John 3:8 the Lord Jesus said, "The wind (speaking of the Holy Spirit) bloweth where it listeth, (or where it wills—the Holy Spirit blows where He wills) and thou hearest the sound thereof, but canst not tell whence it cometh, and whither it goeth: so is every one that is born of the Spirit."

Christ was teaching a very learned man named Nicodemus who came to Him to understand the way of salvation. He was trying to show him that there was a place in God where the Holy Spirit did what He wanted to do.

HOLY SPIRIT'S WILL IN THE OLD TESTAMENT

The first place in recorded Scriptures where we see activity of the Holy Ghost is in Genesis 1:2. It is remarkable to me that on the first page of the Bible, and in the second verse of the Bible we have an activity of the Holy Spirit Himself. It says, "And the earth was without form, and void; and darkness was upon the face of the deep. And the spirit of God moved upon the face of the waters."

There is recorded volitional decision of the Third Person of the Holy Trinity. It was an act of bringing cosmos, beauty, and loveliness out of chaos. The earth was without form and void. God was involved in His creative masterpiece and the Holy Ghost moved in to help Him. The Spirit of God moved on the face of the waters and there came cosmos out of that chaos. The dynamic will of the Holy Spirit challenged the condition, succeeded, and brought it into fruition. We observe the *first record* of the *functioning* of the Holy Spirit.

The Holy Spirit has moved from the beginning of time upon this earth and in eternity also, but in these last days we are living in what is called the Dispensation of the Holy Spirit. You and I should know more about the Holy Spirit than they did in those days because this is His dispensation.

Jesus said, "If I go away, I will send Him unto you." The Holy Spirit is special to us and **we should understand His will.**

His will is the same as the will of the Lord Jesus. The Holy Spirit is absolutely and completely, wonderfully and gloriously submitted unto the Lord Jesus Christ, our Saviour.

Genesis 6:3 says, "And the LORD said, My spirit shall not always strive with man..."

Here we see the Holy Ghost, by His own will, volitionally, creating limits in which He would beg or persuade man to walk in the ways and commandments of Elohim, the mighty God. God said, "I want you to live right, I want you to live good, and I send My Holy Spirit to guide and to direct." Volitionally, the Holy Spirit said, "I will not always beg, I will not always strive, I will not always urge men to serve God." No wonder the Bible says in Ephesians 4:30, "Grieve not the holy Spirit of God..." He can be grieved. Maybe that also is in the area of will, because if a man does not will to grieve others he will not grieve them.

In the first instance we find the Holy Spirit bringing cosmos to the earth. In the second instance we find Him pleading with men, and volitionally saying. "I will not always do this; I'm doing it now but I will not always do this."

The Spirit possesses a willpower of saying His grace and help would go only so far, and no farther.

HOLY SPIRIT'S WILL IN THE NEW TESTAMENT

Acts 5:1-3 says, "But a certain man named Ananias, with Sapphira his wife, sold a possession, And kept back part of the price, his wife also being privy to it, and brought a certain part, and laid it at the apostles' feet. But Peter said, Ananias, why hath Satan filled thine heart to lie to the Holy Ghost, and to keep back part of the price of the land?"

The Holy Ghost willed capital punishment upon Ananias and Sapphira for lying to deity, for lying to the Most High God. He knew everything; they could not lie to Him.

The incident brought great respect to God, and to the church in Jerusalem.

I have witnessed the judgment of the Holy Ghost in my own lifetime. I was conducting a meeting in a town in Arkansas and I especially urged a young man to give his heart to the Lord Jesus. The Holy Spirit was tugging at his will. There were tears in his eyes, but he would not do it. He said, "No, I will not do it." He became very angry in church. Because his sister became a Christian he abused her, and led her out of the church roughly, saying, "Come out of this place; you do not need this kind of religion."

A couple of days later he was plowing in a field when lightning came out of a clear sky and hit him and drove his body into the ground. They found his shoe 30 yards away and it was completely torn, as if someone had taken a knife and cut it to pieces.

You just cannot forsake God and get away with it, because the Holy Ghost has a ministry of bringing people to God.

The Holy Ghost wills to guide the church.

The Bible says that as the disciples were fasting and praying, "the Holy Spirit said, Separate me Barnabas and Saul for the work whereunto I have called them." (Acts 13:2)

The Holy Spirit volitionally endorsed the missionaries to go forth, and therefore, they were sent forth by the strength and the power and the guidance of the Holy Ghost. That is what God desires in His church today. The Holy Spirit is wanting to guide the church. The church in rebellion of the Holy Spirit can get into big trouble, big sorrow, big heartache, and big problems by grieving the Holy Spirit. He is a person and He has a will.

The will of the Holy Ghost is to carry out the desires of the Father. His will is whatever the Father says will be done. His will is to carry out the words and desires of the Lord Jesus. His will is to enrich the church. The will of the Holy Spirit is to anoint. It is the will of the Holy Spirit to come down upon us. It is the will of the Holy Spirit to come down upon the total church. It is the will of the Holy Spirit to come down upon missions.

You say, "But can't the Holy Spirit perform His will without me?" Not against your will. There are denominations that do not desire for the Holy Spirit to work; they are afraid of the Holy Spirit. It is a sad situation to be living in the dispensation of the Holy Spirit and afraid for Him to operate, to function, and to do the things that He has been sent to do.

We all need to say, **"Holy Ghost, my will is flowing with your will** because your will flows with the Father, and **I am flowing with the Father through you."**

The Holy Spirit wills to anoint persons. The Holy Spirit grants gifts to persons. I Corinthians 12:11 says, "But all these worketh that one and the selfsame Spirit, dividing to every man severally as he will."

5

THE WILL OF ANGELS

You may have thought that angels can do as they please and that they are all perfect. But this is not true. Angels have volitional powers just like you have. Angels have transgressed just like humans have because they have a will.

ANGELS WERE CREATED WITH WILL

We will begin back in the Old Testament in Judges 13:16, "And the angel of the LORD said unto Manoah, Though thou detain me, I will not eat of thy bread..." This angel was showing Manoah that he had a will. He could will not to do this or that.

Angels are created beings; they have no navel; they were not born of a woman. Genesis 1:1, "In the beginning God created the heaven and the earth."

This Almighty God, in His select wisdom, created angels as servants and messengers. They are for Him and they possess willpower. **They do not have to serve God.** They may serve God or they can rebel, whichever they will.

Angels are superintelligent creatures, beyond man. They have the knowledge of two worlds, the spirit world and the physical world. They are two-world creatures. Sometimes the wall of partition is broken down and you can see angels. Angels can talk to God and they can talk with man. **God designed angels and gave them superpowers of decision to decide** on special factors. He did this because He wants to merit their love.

ANGELS WILL TO WORSHIP

A beautiful look into the angelic world is in Isaiah 6:1-6, "In the year that king Uzziah died I saw also the Lord sitting upon a throne, high and lifted up, and his train filled the temple. Above it stood the seraphims: each one had six wings; with twain he covered his face, and with twain he covered his feet, and with twain he did fly. And one cried unto another, and said, Holy, holy, holy, is the LORD of hosts: the whole earth is full of his glory. And the posts of the door moved at the voice of him that cried, and the house was filled with smoke. Then said I, Woe is me! for I am undone; because I am a man of unclean lips, and I dwell in the midst of a people of unclean lips: for mine eyes have seen the King, the LORD of hosts. Then flew one of the seraphims unto me, having a live coal in his hand, which he had taken with the tongs from off the altar."

Here we find angels in worship before the throne crying, "Holy, holy, holy, is the LORD of hosts." They were worshiping volitionally **because they wanted to,** because they liked to, because they enjoy it. They are smiling big and singing magnificently unto the Lord. They did this with their will—they willed to do it.

ANGELS WILL TO PROTECT

Psalms 34:7 says, "The angel of the LORD encampeth round about them that fear him, and delivereth them."

Here we find that an angel by his willpower protects good people, righteous people, holy people. You can believe the Bible or not believe the Bible—that is your prerogative, of course.

I could relate stories of how angels have protected missionaries. Wicked men have come to destroy missionaries on the field and the next day would say, "We would like to see the army that was around your compound last night. We saw men 10 ft. tall walking all around your place and we were afraid to hurt you."

If God would open your spiritual eyes you might be amazed at what is there, and thank God for his protecting power by his angels.

ANGELS WILL TO HARVEST SOULS

The angels will bring in the final spiritual harvest. This reaches into the future, but it shows you that the **angels have a will to do things for God.**

In Matthew 12:39 we read, "But he answered and said unto them, An evil and adulterous generation seeketh after a sign; and there shall no sign be given to it, but the sign of the prophet Jonas." Then Jesus continues by saying the angels will bring in the harvest of God.

ANGELIC WILL AND PROPHECY

Angels brought prophecy to man. Daniel 9:21 says, "Yea, whiles I was speaking in prayer, even the man Gabriel, whom I had seen in the vision at the beginning, being caused to fly swiftly, touched me about the time of the evening oblation."

Here we find Gabriel who was sent from God. This means that he had a will, and that he was obedient.

ANGELIC WILL AND HUMANS

We find also that angels can be entertained by humans. Hebrews 13:2 says, "Be not forgetful to entertain strangers: for thereby some have entertained angels unawares." Abraham was *unaware* that the visitors that came to his tent were angels. He thought they were regular people. He made a feast for them but later discovered the angels had a message from God.

My mother believed we entertained angels in our home and she gave reasons for that.

Angels have been, and are, very influential persons functioning by their will. They will to do what God asks them to do.

6

THE WILL OF DEMONS

Demons have **intelligent wills.** They know and understand what they are doing. They are doing what they are doing very deliberately. Many times there is a battle of wills. This was true not only in the Lord Jesus in His battle of wills against the devil, but it is also true in our lives. There is a battle of wills when the devil says, "Do this" and you say, "No." Your mind can say, "I want to do this." Your emotions say, "Oh, that's nice." When your will says, "No," it is all finished. Your **will** is the **strongest part of your soulical being.** You must learn how to yield it to Christ. You must know that it has to be renewed like the renewing of the mind. In order for the will to be what

Jesus wants it to be, it has to be born again, along with the rest of your soulical being.

WILLPOWER CREATED DEMONS

An amazing area of willpower in our universe is that of the devil and demons. The reason they are what they are is because of their will. God did not make them that way. They got that way through their will. Until you know that you have a battle of will between you and the devil, between you and the world, and between you and the flesh, it may be that you will lose every battle. When you know, then you are well armed to be a winner. The demons know both positive and negative aspects of the power of will. They know what it was to follow God, to live for God, and to sing in the heavens. They know what it was for the devil to say, "I will promote myself above the throne of God. I will make myself like the most High." When the devil did that through the power of his will, he lost his divine relationship. In Isaiah 14 he said "I will" five times. Isaiah 14:12-14 says, " How art thou fallen from heaven, O Lucifer, son of the morning! how art thou cut down to the ground, which didst weaken the nations! For thou hast said in thine heart, **I will ascend** into heaven, **I will exalt** my throne above the stars of God. **I will sit** also upon the mount of the congregation, in the sides of the north: **I will ascend** above the heights of the clouds; **I will be** like the most High."

That is history's masterpiece of arrogance. Nowhere in the universe will you find arrogance equal to that. Here was a created being who, through his own will inside of him, said, "I will be greater than the one who created me." The created ones cannot be as great as the Creator. That is not possible. A wristwatch will never be as great as the man who made it. That watch can keep good time and do a lot of things, but it cannot be as great as the one who created it. You are a person created by God and you can never be as great as God. He created you; He conceived you; He designed you; He made you. It is not intelligent to think that one day you will be bigger than God.

This archangel named Lucifer made

five astounding statements of will. He was moving forth not in taste, not in emotion, and not even in intellect. He was moving in willpower.

DEMONIC WILL IN EDEN

The second step in the battle of the wills took place in the Garden of Eden. Satan deceived man in the first encounter. Man was entrapped in the Garden by Satan's willful fall. Why would Adam willfully have eaten, knowing God's will? He knew that it was God's will that he should not eat of the tree. Yet he willed to eat the fruit. So he willfully decided to be like someone else when he could have been like God. In the first encounter of will on Planet Earth, we find that **Satan** by his will **entrapped man,** and caused **man** to **leave the will of God** and to serve the will of the devil.

DEMONIC WILL TODAY

How does the devil come against believers to hurt them today? In John 10:10 Jesus says, "The thief (that is the devil) cometh not, but for to steal, and to kill, and to destroy..."

When the devil comes against you, he comes to do three things. He comes to steal from you. That is what he did to Eve and Adam in the Garden. **He stole** from them **their willpower** and **their desire to walk with God.**

Not only does the devil steal, but he comes to kill and destroy. The devil is a killer. The Bible says that he was a murderer from the beginning; he is a destroyer of life. The only way he can do it is by hitting you in the willpower. If he can break your will down, then you will be like Eve. His system has always been the same. It is a battle of the wills.

You will have a battle of the wills every day. At church time you will have a battle of the wills. "Will I go to church or will I stay home?" That is a battle of your will inside of you. It is not a battle of your emotions. It is not a battle of your mind. It is a battle of the will. If you do not obey the divine and spiritual part of your will, you will be like Satan. The devil seeks to hurt your will and to destroy your will if he possibly can.

7

THE WILL OF HUMANKIND

God created Adam, the first person, the first human, the first earthling. God created him of the earth, so when he dies he goes back to where he came from. He did not come from mixing some chemical acids.

THREE DIMENSIONAL MAN

God made man, at the time of creation, a three-dimensional personality. Neither psychology nor psychiatry realize it yet; humanism will never understand it at all.

Everything in this universe initially perfect is indelibly **stamped with a three.** God is Father, Son, and Holy Spirit—the three function as one.

Man is a spirit, soul, and body—functioning as one.

The will is one-third of the human soulical personality which is one-third of the total personality of the total person. Your soulical parts are made up of your mind, your emotions, and your will by which you relate to other humans.

When God created man and placed him in Eden, He said, "There is one tree here that belongs to Me. The other trees and their fruit belong to you."

In every home it is the same. The Father says, "This is mine." Mama says, "This is mine, and son, this is yours." Inevitably the little boy wants Papa's, and Mama's and his. This was the problem in the Garden of Eden. God said, "We are partners. I built the whole scheme of things. I'll make you the president and you are in charge. There is one tree here, the tree of the Knowledge of Good and Evil, you are not to touch." *That tree was to build character in Adam.* It was up to Adam to operate positively in his will to obey God, or negatively to disobey Him.

I Corinthians 15:45 says, "And so it is

written, The first man Adam was made a living soul; the last Adam was made a quickening spirit.'' This scripture describes the difference between Adam of the Garden of Eden and Jesus, born to be Christ.

You and I are naturally the seed of Adam. We are supernaturally the seed of Jesus Christ, the seed of God. The Bible says that when you believe upon the Lord, ''Now you are the sons of God.'' As soon as you believe, you are a son of God. You move into another realm and your total abilities, spirit, soul, and body, relate to God, to things spiritual. When your will is obedient to God, then the emotional and mental areas of your life will fall in line, because the will has power to discipline.

But the will first has to be regenerated. In Adam we become a living soul, but in Christ we become a quickening spirit. So we are twice sons; we are sons of Adam naturally and we are sons of the Spirit supernaturally. As the sons of God, our wills have been cleansed, purified, and renewed.

The Bible is the solitary source of knowledge to draw the truth regarding the mystery of the inner workings of the human person. I am sorry that philosophers do not know this. They go everywhere except to the true source to find out about man. Hebrews 4:12, "For the word of God is quick, and powerful, and sharper than any two-edged sword, piercing even to the dividing asunder of soul and spirit, and of the joints and marrow, and is a discerner of the thoughts and intents of the heart."

HUMAN LIFE DOMINATED BY WILL

The human will functions from the time of birth. Possibly you did not realize this, but doctors know. When a woman is in labor the baby assists in delivery; he brings himself out.

In childhood when a child says, "No, no, no," he is exercising willpower, not physical power, and not his emotional power.

At the time of his spiritual conversion and born-again experience, man comes into a tremendous situation of will. **He wills to receive Christ as his Savior** and becomes a new creature in Christ Jesus. His process of will is changed.

Will is also involved in your receiving the Holy Spirit. There are some people who have the will to be saved but do not have the will to go further in God. Their will seems to cease at the point of salvation. The Bible explicitly tells us in I John that there are three witnesses to God in the earth and they are the blood, the water and the Spirit. Some people stop at *the blood.* Some people stop at *the blood and water.* Some get *all the way through* to the spirit. When the three function, you will be what God desires for you to be.

Not only is the will powerful in receiving the Holy Spirit, but also in receiving and operating in the gifts and ministries of the Holy Spirit. The willpower is there. If you do not will to accept, it will not work. If you do not will to have them, they will not operate. **Will** is a source of **desire.** It is a source of **hope.**

The human **will** is a **decision maker.** It is a willful activity. A non-decision is also a decision. When your will refuses to function and make a decision, it is making a decision.

An unconscious decision is a fruit of the will. When you do things unconsciously, your will has been disciplined in that it will act under certain circumstances and certain influences; therefore, an unconscious decision is a fruit of the human will.

It was Eve's will that caused her to fall. It was not Eve's body—her five senses. It was her will. When her tempter Satan said, "Listen. You will be great and you will be equal with God if you will eat this," her will within her said, "I will be as great as God. I will be like the Most High." It was her will that caused her downfall.

WILL IS A GIFT

The human will is a gift from God. The greatest experience of human achievement is in performing the will of God. The human **will** is **immortal.** You will have it after this life. You will keep your will in eternity and those who go to heaven will possess a will to serve God and to enjoy heaven. Those who go to hell will have a will.

SOVEREIGN WILL

The human will is sovereign. God will not violate it. He created you and made you a responsible person. You cannot blame God for the actions of your will. You are the one in charge. You are the one who holds the wheel and you do the driving. God will not stop your will. If He did, you would not be a human anymore. You would be some kind of a creature without a will.

Satan cannot violate your will because he does not have the proper power to do it. God made the human will so strong until Satan has to ask permission for you to grant him your will. You determine your decisions and then your guardian angel can act for you. You first have to stress your own willpower, and you have to move in a certain direction before your angel can act on your behalf. Angels are not permitted to control human will. Only **you** can control your own will.

Demons seek to control your destiny by your will. In their attempt to control the human will or to weaken the will, demons can make sin attractive and desirable.

They try to break down the willpower by saying, "This won't hurt you; that won't hurt you; this won't take you to hell." They are seeking to break down your will to serve the Lord Jesus. Demons use deceit and trickery against the human will.

The human will, *if protected,* must be living in the Word of God and in the worship of God. **It must be humbled before the Lord.** Then the human soul will certainly be victorious.

When you say, "Thy will be done" it is a spiritual act and not an Adamic act. **Adam actually put his will against God's will.** I Corinthians 15:22 says, "For as in Adam all die, even so in Christ shall all be made alive."

Adam deliberately, volitionally, **willfully rebelled** against God.

The **Lord Jesus Christ willfully** and volitionally **submitted** His will to God the Father. That is the difference between the two.

THE REDEEMED WILL

In the new life of the second Adam, we see the stratagems of spiritual life and spiritual warfare. We are taught from the Bible of the Lord Jesus; we are taught by the Holy Spirit; we learn how to battle successfully against the devil in the world of will; we also learn how to worship God in the world of will. There is real danger in a lack of teaching. There has been little teaching on will.

The unconverted human will of a child, screaming, kicking, yelling, is exercising willpower that is uncontrolled and undisciplined. The child is not using his mind. There is no pain in the child's body, yet he wills to scream uncontrollably. His **ego wants attention.** The child must learn to bring his will to God.

The **converted man** is the opposite. His will and total soulical parts underwent an amazing and miraculous **change at conversion.** The rebellion against God ceased to be.

DISCERNING WILL

Possibly the supreme message of this hour is the comprehension between what is **God's will,** what is **man's will,** and what is the **devil's will!**

The devil wants to take us all to Armageddon and kill us.

Man does not know what he wants to do. He flutters around like a butterfly. He thinks he wants all kinds of sensual accomplishments and to be pleased in his senses. That does not satisfy him. Man is an immortal creature and cannot fully be satisfied without loving, and praising and honoring God. Only by spirit can man know spiritual reality of God's will. Most people have no idea of God's will. We use the word so quickly, "What is God's will?" We say "will" so quickly until we do not even hear it, but we need to say it a lot slower, W-I-L-L because it is so important. It is impossible to have spiritual development and maturity without an understanding of the different functions of the human will. We have **many Christians** today who have come to know the Lord Jesus Christ and **are living in their soulical part of their will** that is in rebellion.

Until a Christian can differentiate between God's will and his own will, he will most likely be living in the lower realm of his own will and not in the spiritual realm—the upper realm of God's will. It is impossible to continually walk in God's will until we know what God's will is. To the natural man it is a mystery. In Matthew 11:25 Jesus said, "I thank thee, O Father, Lord of heaven and earth, because thou hast hid these things from the wise and prudent, and hast revealed them unto babes." You and I know truth that others do not know. We understand things about the human person that others do not understand. We recognize that man is not just clay and air, but that he is divine and that within him are mysteries such as the human mind, the human emotions, and the human will that God has planted within him.

DOING GOD'S WILL

Ephesians 5:17, "Wherefore be ye not unwise, but **understanding what the will of the Lord is.**" What does God will in your natural life here on this earth? God has a plan for your life dominated by will and He would like for you to let that will be strong in Him, in His great power."

Ephesians 6:6, "Not with eye-service, as men-pleasers; but as the servants of Christ, **doing the will of God from the heart.**" Man can do as he pleases. God is not going to overwhelm him. If you do not will an action a certain way, it will never be that way. God is asking, requesting, a will submitted to Him. It is the will of God for the gospel to be preached in all the world. If you wish to do the will of God, accept the challenge of the Great Commission. Your mind and emotions may not want to, but your will is the dominating factor and it is **your will that can cause you to rise up and be the person that God wants you to be.**

Man also worships by his will. In Matthew 6:10, Jesus said that when you pray say, "Thy kingdom come. Thy will be done in earth, as it is in heaven."

One day this will be fulfilled. The Lord Jesus shall reign for a thousand years upon this earth and perform the will of God. The earth will function as God intended it to in the first place. Christians will be reigning with Him performing the will of God.

If you today will say, "God, I am interested in performing your will in my life, in my family, in my church, and in my country," the will of God will be revealed and accomplished.